... in a

... the

... y to
... rsal

... *Booklist*

... ory
... the 13-
... emotions
powerfully . . . To a budding genre . . . this book is a
welcome addition' *Kirkus Review*

'a deeply moving first novel . . . powerful and
uplifting.' Sheila Wood, *Bookseller*

'a *tour de force*.' *The Scotsman*

'a stunning book in the tradition of Sylvia Plath's
The Bell Jar . . . the first by Sones, whose allusive and
startling poems evoke an ordinary teenager's
shattered world with powerful intensity.'
Books Magazine

'This is a haunting and unforgettable first book.'
Armadillo

'a complex, satisfying narrative with the texture of a
novel.' *TES*

Also by Sonya Sones

What my mother doesn't know:
A story of love and confusion

STOP PRETENDING

what

happened

when

my

big

sister

went

crazy

SONYA SONES

Dolphin Paperbacks

Excerpt from *Anne Frank: the Diary of a Young Girl*
by Anne Frank. Copyright 1952 by Otto H. Frank
used by permission of Doubleday, a division of Random House, Inc.

First published in the USA 1999 by
HarperCollins Publishers
First published in Great Britain in 2001
by Orion Children's Books
This edition first published 2002 by Dolphin Paperbacks
an imprint of Orion Children's Books
a division of the Orion Publishing Group Ltd
Orion House
5 Upper St Martin's Lane
London WC2H 9EA

A catalogue record for this book is
available from the British Library

Printed in Great Britain by
Clays Ltd, St Ives plc

ISBN 1 84255 075 6

to

my

sister

ACKNOWLEDGMENTS

I would like to offer my heartfelt thanks to my teacher, Myra Cohn Livingston, for setting me on the path to writing this book, and to the Society of Children's Book Writers and Illustrators for awarding me a Work-In-Progress Grant.

I owe an enormous debt of gratitude to my children for graciously sharing me with my computer, and to my husband, Bennett, my biggest fan, for listening so eagerly and advising so well.

I am deeply grateful to my agent, Steven Malk, for catapulting me into a new life; to my editor, Alix Reid, for asking all the right questions; and to my critique group and the members of Myra's Master Class, for their many excellent suggestions and for their unflagging enthusiasm for this project, which helped give me the courage to complete it.

STOP PRETENDING

MY WHOLE FAMILY

I can
remember what
things were like before she
got sick: my whole family climbed
into

the big
hammock on the
moondappled beach, wove
ourselves together, and swayed
as one.

MY SISTER'S
CHRISTMAS EVE BREAKDOWN

One day
she was my big
sister, so normal and
well-behaved, the next she was a
stranger

rushing
out the door to
Midnight Mass, a wild-eyed
Jewish girl wearing only a
nightgown.

One day
he was my dad,
so calm and quiet and
in control, the next he was a
stranger

dragging
my big sister
away from the door, up
the stairs, screaming so loud that my
ears stung.

One day
she was my mom,
so reliable and good in
a crisis, the next she was a
stranger

standing
stock still with her
hands clamped over her mouth
and her eyes squeezed shut, not even
breathing.

That day
I sank into
the wall, wondering what
these three people were doing in
my house

and I
shouted that they
had to stop, even though
I wasn't supposed to talk to
strangers.

THREE A.M. THAT SAME NIGHT

She hasn't gone to Mass,
hasn't gone to sleep,
hasn't stopped to catch her breath—
she can't stop talking.

She's showing me her stuff,
tons of stuff she bought,
stuff she bought this afternoon
when she went shopping.

Our bedroom's filled with bags,
way too many bags,
bags crammed full with too much stuff,
they're overflowing.

She's emptying them out:
fifty bars of soap,
feather dusters, Ping-Pong balls,
a ski mask, fishbowls,

twelve pairs of sexy shoes
(the kind she never wears),

stationery monogrammed
with wrong initials.

I'm huddled on my bed,
wrapped up in my quilt,
listening to Sister rave
on and on and

just outside the door
angry whispers rise.
Trying not to let us hear,
our parents fight.

I'm huddled on my bed,
rocking in my quilt,
wishing I could fall asleep
and end this nightmare.

NEAR DAWN

She's quiet now,
sitting there
with her eyes glued
to the blank screen
of the television,

totally
engrossed.

HOSPITALIZED

Sister's in the psycho ward
and when I visit, I glance toward
the other patients' twisted faces,
quaking fingers,
frightened eyes,
wishing I could somehow break her out of here . . .

Then Sister starts to scream at Mother,
telling her how much she hates her,
begging her to stop the voices
chattering inside her skull.
I'm feeling sick,
the air's too thick . . .

Suddenly I'm running, stumbling,
Sister's demons chasing after,
leering, laughing,
right behind me
lurching at my heels
remind me:

I could have been the one.
Run, Sister, run!

QUESTIONS

When my friends ask where she is,
I tell them
she's in the hospital.

When they ask why,
I shrug
and say she's sick.

When they ask what kind of sick,
my cheeks flame up
and I change the subject.

THIN SKIN

Sometimes
I worry that
the truth will break out all
over my face, like a fresh crop
of zits.

NEW YEAR'S EVE

No party.
No dancing.
No confetti.
No balloons.
No streamers.
No Times Square ball dropping.
No resolutions.
No "Auld Lang Syne."

No
nothing.

WHAT IT'S LIKE

When I arrive
she's on all fours
rocking back and forth,
wearing a blouse over her nightgown.

Leaping up,
she pulls the curtains open
to show me her view.
Staring past the bars on her window,
she shudders
and yanks the curtains shut.

Whipping around,
she points to her mirror,
shrouded with a sheet.
"I had to, Cookie,"
she says with a quick laugh.
"I didn't look like me."

Then she freezes
with hands outstretched,
like rabbits freeze when danger's near,
and all at once

she throws herself into a chair.
She says this chair
controls the room
and all her thoughts
and all mine, too.

I don't
know what
to say.

She catches me checking my watch
and glares at me,
hissing, "Don't run away so fast."
But I stand up.
And when we hug goodbye,
neither of us
wants to let go.

I WONDER

Does the
man who wanders
the neighborhood, wearing
three heavy overcoats in the
swelter

of the
summer, have a
little sister who lies
awake at night wondering where
he is?

MIDNIGHT SWING

When I can't fall asleep
I sneak out to the yard
and climb onto the swing
that's attached to a branch
of the sweet scented pine.

As I glide through the night
and I hang back my head
I see stars and a moon
that's following me
through the evergreen trees.

And I fly on my swing
through the midnight ice cold
as the swirling white clouds
of my own frozen breath
brush my tingling cheeks.

And my nightgown wafts up
and my hair billows out
as I float through the air
and there's only the sound
of the dark whooshing past.

And my thoughts drift to you
on a day long ago
when my legs were too short
so you helped me climb up
and you taught me to pump.

PAPER DOLL

I can remember
watching you
while you sat on the hooked rug
in our bedroom

drawing her
heart-shaped face
and curlicue hairdo,
her delicate arms, legs, and feet,

then coloring her in
with such care
and holding her up to the window to trace
so the clothes would fit just right

on that perfect little paper doll
that you'd made
just
for me.

IN THE MORNING

there's
this golden moment
when the sun
licks through the gauze
fluttering at my window
warming my eyelids to opening

this golden moment
when I'm not yet awake enough
to remember
that there are things
I would rather
forget

BREAKFAST TIME

Your chair
is so empty
that I want to leap up
from the table and run out of
the room.

NOTHING HAS CHANGED

Walking to school
with Molly and Kate,
scuffling along through the snow,
we joke about Molly's crush on Matt
and race to the corner like kids.

When I'm walking to school
with Molly and Kate,
and we're all singing
that new song
from the radio,

I can pretend
that things are fine,
that nothing has changed,
that everything's just
like it used to be

before.

WONDERING
THROUGH THE HALLS AT SCHOOL

Would he smile at me in quite that way
if he knew my sister was insane?
Or would he look at me
like I was weird?

I wonder if she'd be as nice
if she found out that Sis had flipped.
Would she still be willing to be my friend, or
would she drop me faster than the speed of light?

If I told them that my sister's nuts,
they might *act* sympathetic,
but behind my back
would everyone laugh?

If I let them all know,
would they go?

IN ART CLASS

I'm drawing my sister
with saucers for eyes.
The saucers are spinning out sparks.

I'm drawing my mother
with zippers for eyes.
The zippers are zipped up tight.

I'm drawing my father
with windows for eyes.
The windows are broken and cracked.

I'm drawing myself
without any eyes
at all.

INSTEAD OF STUDYING
DURING STUDY HALL

I'm thinking about when I was five,
when my sister tried to convince me
that I was adopted.
She pointed out that no one else
in our family had green eyes,
no one else had such big ears,
or such wavy brown hair and olive skin.
She said I must be part Italian
and started calling me Cookachini.

At the time,
my parents had to show me
my birth certificate
just to get me to stop bawling.
But now, after all these years,
I've finally figured it out:
My sister is the one who was adopted.
My parents just kept it a secret, that's all.
She's not a thing like the rest of us.

She's not my real sister.
I don't have
any
of the same genes as her,
not one single same gene,
not one
single
insane
gene.

AT LUNCH

Everybody's sitting around telling jokes.
I haven't giggled this much
in ages.

Then Kate says, "Okay. Okay. I've got one:
Which path does the mental patient take
to get through the forest?"

and they all ask, "Which path?"
and Kate says, "The psycho path!"
and everyone bursts out laughing,

except me.

THOUGHTS DURING ENGLISH CLASS

They're looking at me
like they know.
I wonder if it shows
on my face.

Was that a smirk on Sarah's lips?
Has the word gotten out?
What could Liz and Beth and Ariel
be whispering about?

Did I give it away
with my eyes?
They're looking at me
like they know.

FIRST FLIGHT

Today
I helped
Mrs. Murr's kindergarten class
set their butterfly free.

It darted out
through the gap that they'd made
in the green netting
of the cage,

then found the breeze
and fluttered away
dizzily
into the sky.

I'd never seen
the first flight
of a butterfly before.
I didn't know I'd feel like crying.

WHAT WOULD HAPPEN IF

Walking home from school
with Molly and Kate,
listening to them chatter
about the C minus
Molly got in math
and about how her parents
are going to kill her
when they find out

and about how Kate
simply can't decide
whether to wear her pink dress
or her black dress
to the dance with Tim
this Friday,

wishing I *had* a Tim
to take me to the dance,
wishing
I even felt
like dancing,

I say, "Why don't you just wear
that great little red dress, Kate?
The one you wore to the last dance."
"That old thing?" she gasps.
"Are you out of your mind?"

I blink at her stupidly,
wishing I could say,
"No, I'm not. But my sister is,"
and wondering
what would happen
if I did.

SINCE SISTER'S BEEN SICK

four in the afternoon
home from school
I trudge upstairs
peer through Mother's bedroom door:
shades drawn
airless

I mumble "hello"
no "hello"
no "how was school?"
just
the rumpled figure
snoring in the unmade bed
theme song from
Days of Our Lives
droning

I rush past
into my room
flick on the radio
and turn the volume
way
up

SNAPSHOT

I'm looking at the photo
of when you were eight,
holding me when I was one.
It looks like we're having fun.
I'm grinning at you
like I think you're great.
You didn't look crazy
at all back then.
I wish you could be eight
again.

FOUND AND LOST

I can remember the day
I fell asleep under the bed
and everyone thought I was lost.

While the rest of them
rushed off
to search the neighborhood,

you wandered through the house
calling out,
"Cookieeeee, we're going to the pierrrrr!"

Your words woke me
and I scrambled out
from under the bed.

I remember feeling
startled
by the enormous hug you gave me . . .

When I was lost,
you were the one
who found me,

now you're the one
who's lost,
and I can't find you anywhere.

THINGS WOULD BE DIFFERENT

If I
had a dog, I
could hold him when I felt
like this, and he'd lick the salt off
my cheeks.

THE PHONE RINGS

It's my sister.
She tells me
that she'll talk to me as long as she likes.
That no one can stop her.
That no one would dare.

She tells me
that the telephone's on fire
but I shouldn't worry because it doesn't hurt.
She tells me that when I'm nineteen, like her,
things will really pick up.

She tells me that her fingernails
are swelling,
that her heart isn't beating,
that the stool in the phone booth is melting,
that the light bulb is twice as big as a man's head.

It's my sister.
I can't just hang up.

MY SUPPER THEORIES AS TO WHY

Maybe
it was the fierce
crunch of my father's teeth
chomping on those raw carrots that
freaked her . . .

Maybe
it was the smell
of the cigarettes and
sour pickles Mother inhaled
nightly . . .

Maybe
it was the din
of silence at suppers . . .

Or maybe it was something that
I did.

APOLOGIES

I'm sorry
I borrowed your favorite sweater
without asking
and then got that ink stain on it
that wouldn't ever come out.

I'm sorry
I lied about it afterwards,
when you asked me
if I knew how it got there
and I swore I had no idea.

And I lied about your goldfish, too.
He didn't just die a mysterious death like I said,
that week when you were away
on that Girl Scout trip.
I forgot to feed him.

I shouldn't have pretended
your piano playing made me gag
and I shouldn't have read your diary,
even if you did
leave it lying around on your bed.

And I never should have
told on you that night
when you were grounded
and you snuck out the window
to go to that dance with Nick.

And I wish
I hadn't said
I hated you
just because you yelled at me
when you found out what I did.

I'm sorry for
every
single
terrible
thing.

TO THE RESCUE

When the nurse
isn't looking
I'll steal her keys,
take your hand,
unlock the elevator door
and pull you in behind me.

We'll hold our breath
until the doors slide open
and then,
very casually, we'll stroll past the guard,
through the lobby
and right out the front door.

On the sidewalk,
I'll take you by the shoulders,
look into your eyes,
say the perfect words
and suddenly
you'll be cured.

You'll smile at me
through your tears
and call me your hero.
You'll tell me
that everything
will be all right now

thanks to me.

ENGLISH HOMEWORK: DESCRIBE YOUR BEDROOM

It's not very big, considering I have to share it with my sister. But it *is* very pink: the stripes on the bedspreads, the polka dots on the pillows, the stuffed animals, the curtains, the wastebaskets, the rug, and the flowers on the wallpaper, all pink. (My sister and I wanted yellow, but our mother was in charge of decorating.)

When I sit on my pink bed and look across the room, it's like looking at a rosy reflection in a mirror. There's another pink desk that looks just like mine, another nightstand exactly the same, with the same pink lamp on it, another dresser with pink glass knobs, and sitting on it is the same exact jewelry box, with a little pink ballerina that dances when you open it up.

The only thing missing is another girl sitting on the other pink bed, looking back across the room at me.

SISTER'S ROOM

How can she live
in that puke green room
with only that one barred window
to look out of?

How can she sleep
in that narrow steel bed
on that thin mattress
under those scratchy sheets?

How can she read
by the cold glare
of that fluorescent light on her ceiling?
How can she stand its constant hum?

How can she bear people looking in at her
whenever they feel like it
through that square of chicken-wired glass
in her door?

"The only good thing about this room,"
she tells me with a choked little laugh,
"is that there isn't
one single pink thing in it."

I WISH I MAY, I WISH I MIGHT

There's a big wind tonight,
whipping round the corners
of our house,

skittering the branches
of the maple
against the windowpane,

slamming the screen door
again
and again,

a big wind whisking
the clouds out of the way
to show me the crisp evening star.

There's a big wish tonight,
a star light,
star bright wish,

a wishing
for the wind
to blow my sister home,

home to her bed
that lies empty
next to mine,

home
to me,
to where she belongs.

FEBRUARY 15TH

Imagine having to get into the car
and go skidding across icy streets,
scared to death of crashing,
while listening to your parents
bicker in the front seat.

Imagine climbing out of the car
and marching in silence
up slippery hospital steps,
through a tangle of corridors reeking of Lysol,
to visit someone you've never met,

someone who won't talk to you,
or smile
or even look at you,
someone who just sits there
glaring at the floor.

And imagine
trying to pretend
that it's
not
your birthday.

WHEN WE GO

Usually we go to see her every Sunday
and we stay for about an hour
if she's not doing too bad.

Sometimes my parents just say a quick hello
and leave me alone with her
while they go down the hall to their therapy session.

Sometimes I have too much homework
so I stay home
and my parents go without me.

Sometimes I
just *say*
I have too much homework.

WHAT WE DO

Most of the time
the four of us just sit in the visiting room
and talk,
when we can think of something to talk about.

Sometimes Sister *won't* talk,
so the three of us have a conversation
as if she isn't even there.
Only she is.

Sometimes Sister won't *stop* talking
and we just have to
sit there
and listen.

On a good day, we'll play cards or
maybe a board game,
or Mother might coax Sister over to the piano
to play "Chopsticks."

On a bad day, Sister shoves Mother
off the piano bench
and pounds on the keys
with her fists.

It's better when my parents leave us alone.
Then we usually go into Sister's room and draw.
Her pictures are scary,
but it's easier than talking.

TRYING TO PLAY MONOPOLY

The four of us
sit at the bridge table
in the visiting room on Sunday afternoon
trying to play Monopoly.

Sister keeps rolling the dice
and ignoring the numbers that come up,
moving her thimble,
or whichever piece she feels like,
wherever she feels like moving it,
sometimes to BOARDWALK,
sometimes to GO,
but most of the time directly to JAIL.

It's about as much fun as being stung by a bee,
watching my father squirm in his chair
while Sister keeps sneaking
thousand-dollar bills into her blouse,
and Mother keeps making dumb little jokes,
trying to pretend
like everything's normal.

But I can see the muscle twitching
just slightly
under Mother's left eye.
I can see the film of sweat
forming over Father's upper lip.

When Sister rolls snake eyes,
her own eyes pop
and she leaps from her seat,
grabbing the board
and heaving it into the air,
sending houses and cards flying,
pastel money fluttering to the ground
in slow motion.

My stunned parents stare,
like witnesses at a car crash,
while two orderlies rush over
to whisk my screaming sister
from the room.

MASS PIKE

On the way home from the hospital
my father starts crying so hard
that he has to pull over
by the side of the road,

and we weep with him
while cars filled
with happy families
whiz past.

NO MATTER WHAT

Even if my mother and father
get killed in a car crash
and I have to go stay
with Aunt Frances and Uncle Paul
in New Jersey

and even if
their house burns down
so I get sent to a foster home
and my foster parents are alcoholics
who beat me

and even if
I run away
but I get caught
and the social worker says
I have to go live in an orphanage in Omaha

and even if
when I'm on the airplane
on the way to the orphanage
a terrorist takes over
and makes the pilot land on a deserted island

and even if
the plane crashes
and everyone dies but the terrorist and me
and the island is surrounded
by hungry sharks,

I swear I won't go crazy.

SUNDAY NIGHT

I'm listening to the sounds
of the baseball game
seeping through the wall from the next room

knowing that my father is sitting in there
in the dark
staring at the flickering screen,

too weary to talk
or even to sit in silence
next to someone on the couch.

I'm hating the crack of the bat,
the roar of the fans,
the announcer's stupid voice.

I'm hating these sounds
that remind me
that my dad is in there

with the baseball game,
and I'm in here
alone.

LIFE ON THE WARD

she tells me
that if she wants to watch TV
she has to walk all the way down the corridor
to the patient lounge
hoping that when she gets there
the other patients
are watching what *she* wants to watch

and they never are

she tells me
that if she wants to make a phone call
she has to wait in line
at the phone booth in the hallway

and by the time it's her turn
sometimes she can't even remember
who it was she wanted to call

she tells me
that if she wants something special for dinner
then that's just too bad

I tell her
she has to hurry up and get well

she looks at me
like I'm nuts

HOW I KNOW
WHEN IT'S TIME TO LEAVE

If I stay
any longer
than an hour,
I get this weird feeling
that if I look in the mirror
I'll see that my eyes
have turned into *her* eyes,
my lips
have turned into *her* lips,
and if I speak
my voice will come out sounding
just
like
hers.

THE LOCKED WARD

Lost on the locked ward,
I'm roaming the corridors
crawling with lunatics.

Haunting
the olive drab hallways,
they're watching me,

stalking me,
rocking and drooling.
Who'll show me the door?

I've got to
get out of here
now!

Spotting a nurse,
I'm suddenly sobbing.
She smiles, walking towards me

and holds out her arms,
speaking so soothingly:
"You're looking lost.

Follow me down this hall.
I'll lead you out.
It can be scary. I know."

In only a moment,
we're standing before
a locked elevator door.

"Now where is my key . . . ?"
she ponders aloud.
Something is odd.

Just then, a doctor
walks up and unlocks the door.
Quickly, I hurry aboard.

I turn to thank the nurse.
She winks at me coyly,
and suddenly sticks out her tongue.

Just as the doors close,
I see that she's drooling,
and rocking and rocking and rocking.

REALITEASE

It seems
like Sister is
the crazy one, but what
if it's really the other way
around

and it's
actually
me who's the crazy one,
only I'm so crazy, I think
it's her?

ANOTHER VISIT WITH SISTER

I can feel
my face morphing
when she cocks her head,
lifts her chin,
and with laser eyes
that peer through slits
from beneath brows arched high,
she tries
to determine who I
really
am.

STOP PRETENDING

Stop pretending.
Right this minute.
Don't you tell me
you don't know me.
Stop this crazy act
and show me
that you haven't changed.
Stop pretending
you're deranged.
Stop a minute.
You'll remember things
like they used to be
when you used to read to me
from Dr. Seuss in our backyard.
Stop pretending.
Right this minute.
I'm your sister.
Don't you tell me
you don't know me.

THE TRUTH IS

I don't want to see you.
I dread it.
There.
I've said it.

YOU ARE

Balmy,
bonkers,
daffy,
loco,

loony,
raving,
nutty,
psycho,

buggy,
cuckoo,
batty,
wacko.

You are crazy.

I am not.

IN DR. SAUNDERS' OFFICE

I don't
want to be here.
My parents made me come.
They said I probably

have lots of mixed-up feelings
about my sister being sick
and I'd feel so much better
if I had someone to talk to.

If that's the case
then why don't
they
talk to me?

I'm sitting
in this squeaky leather chair
swiveling
back and forth.

I'll sit here till the hour's up
but I'm not going to say
one
word.

SISTER IN SLUMBERLAND

She's asleep when we come in,
curled up on her bed
with her dirty brown hair
drifting around her face,
her eyelids fluttering with a dream.

It's strange how much she looks like her old self
when her eyes are closed.
Except for her skin.
She used to have the rosiest cheeks.
She didn't even need makeup.

And she used to look
so clean all the time,
with every shining strand
of her hair
perfectly arranged.

She used to look so—
Good.
I used to wish I looked like her.
I used to wish I
was her.

AFTER MIDNIGHT

lying in my bed
thinking about my sister
lying in *her* bed
at the hospital

suddenly seeing
myself lying there
in my sister's bed
alone in the locked-up dark

I try to take a breath
but I can't pull in enough air my
lungs are locked I
try again I
can't

panic rises
grabs me by the throat
tightens its grip
won't let
me go

till I scream

IT'S BEEN FOREVER

Ready or not,
here I come.
I'm so tired
of this dumb game
of hide-and-seek.
Ollee ollee oxen free.
Show yourself.
You're scaring me.
Come out,
come out,
wherever you are.
You've taken this thing
way
too far.

THE YOU I REMEMBER

I
blink

and there you suddenly are,
inhabiting your eyes again,

shining your warmest big-sisterly gaze on me
then slipping away

before we even
have a chance to—

LAST JUNE ON OCEAN AVENUE

You and I
could see a yellow rose,
a teddy bear
and the back of a silver frame
in the bay window
of the house we wished we lived in.

You said,
"If we were up there in that room,
maybe we'd hear the waves crashing,
maybe we'd glance down and see
a girl and her sister looking up at us,
wishing it was *their* summer cottage."

I loved it when you
had thoughts
like that.

You used to
have them
all the time.

LAST JULY, WHEN SISTER
AND I GOT LOST AT THE CAPE

we stayed to watch
the sinking sun
then started back
across the dunes

and lost our way
on miles and miles
of rambling paths
that looked alike

and as the light
drained from the sky
we hurried through
that life-size maze

imagining
how it would feel
to spend the night
all by ourselves

with just the *shushhhhh*
of lapping waves
the far-off cries
of seagull ghosts

and sleep on sand
still warm from sun
with mysteries
surrounding us

and when we found
the parking lot
we weren't so sure
that we were glad

LAST AUGUST AT NANTASKET BEACH

Strolling with my sister
on the crowded boardwalk
under stars and sizzling neon,

inhaling the pink scent
of spun sugar, the salty tangs
of popcorn and beer,

the beats
of a hundred different radios
passed us by.

A boy with sunblond hair
grinned big and white
in our direction

whistling,
"Who witt,
who wooooooooo!"

I nudged her
and whispered proudly,
"That guy just whistled at you!"

She cocked her head
and looked at me
in a way she never had before

then flashed me a smile
and whispered back,
"That guy whistled at *you*."

My first time ever.
If she hadn't told me,
I'd never have known.

PHOTO REALISM

When I look at the little strip of goofy pictures
that Sister and I took
in that photo booth
just a few days before she broke down,

I can't see even a hint,
not the slightest flicker
that any of this
was going to happen.

Did the camera
somehow miss it,
or wasn't it there
to see?

SAINT PATRICK'S DAY

Dr. Saunders was wearing
this dumb green polka-dotted dress today.
I came in and sat down
and, as usual,
I didn't say anything.

We both just sat there
not saying anything,
until this rowdy bunch of guys walked by
right outside the window
singing "When Irish Eyes Are Smiling."

Dr. Saunders asked me,
"Do you like that tune?"
and then I don't know why this happened,
but I found myself telling her all about
how my father sings exactly one song,

this silly little song
called "Dear Little Buttercup"
and how he sings it
in this really
high voice

and how it always used to
make my sister and me
fall on the floor laughing
when he did it and
how he hasn't sung that song in months.

Then these tears
just started flooding out of me,
but Dr. Saunders didn't say anything,
she just sat there and watched me
with this really sympathetic look on her face.

Now I'm sitting outside her office
waiting for my mother to pick me up
and my eyes are all red and puffy.
Next week,
I'll bring my sunglasses.

MOLLY, KATE AND ME

Last Thursday
I finally got the courage up
to tell Molly and Kate
about my sister.
They were so nice about it.
So understanding.

At first.

But now they ignore me,
and every morning
when I walk to school
I can see them up ahead,
shoulder to cold shoulder,
freezing me out.

THOUGHTS
DURING SCIENCE CLASS

People say
that Audrey Becker's
odd.

They say
that her mother
chain-smokes cigars.

They say
that Michael Kinney's uncle
got sent to jail
for robbing the First National Bank.

They say
that Jamie Bennett
saw Eve Chessman's dad
kissing Jeremy Finn's mom
behind the bleachers
in Albermarle Park.

They say
that Danny Sullivan's brother
is an alcoholic
and that's why
he totaled his car
and has to wear that neck brace.

I wonder what they say about me.

MINUS

Last night
Sister wasn't there
to help me study for my math test.

Father tried to fill in
but he's never been as good at math
as her.

This morning
I'm sitting here
taking the test

but the numbers on the page
keep scrambling
in my head

and the only equation
I really understand is:
$4 - 1 = 0$.

IN ENGLISH CLASS

We've been reading
The Diary of Anne Frank.

Anne called her diary Kitty
because she said
she wanted it to be her friend.
She wrote:
"I hope I shall be able to confide in you completely
as I have never been able to do in anyone before."

If I had a diary, I'd call it Meg,
after that girl in *A Wrinkle in Time*
who saves her brother at the end of the book
just by loving him,
just by saying "I love you, Charles!"
over and over again.

I wish that would work
on my sister.

DURING HISTORY CLASS

I notice
Molly scribbling something
on a scrap of paper.
She passes it to Lindsey
when Mrs. Ray isn't looking.

Lindsey reads it and giggles,
peeking in my direction.
She passes it to Jessica
who stifles a laugh and passes it to Rachel
who grins and passes it to Megan.

Megan's sitting right next to me.
She reads it and snickers
but doesn't pass it to me.
Instead she crumples it up
and stuffs it into her desk.

When Megan gets called up
to read her report to the class,
I sneak my hand into her desk
and pull out
the note.

It says:

COOKIE'S SISTER IS CUCKOO.

And underneath the words
is a drawing of a girl
with her eyes crossed
and her hair looking like she just
stuck her finger into an electric outlet.

I cram the note
into my pocket
and pray for the bell to ring
so I can escape
before anyone sees my face.

I hate them all.

IN FRENCH CLASS

Madame V
begins the lesson
by reading aloud the first stanza
of a famous French poem:

Il pleure dans mon cœur
Comme il pleut sur la ville;
Quelle est cette langueur
Qui pénètre mon coeur?

Then she looks up
and without any warning
she calls on *me* to translate it.
I swallow hard, and try:

"It's raining in my heart
like it's raining in the city.
What is this sadness
that pierces my heart?"

Saying these words out loud,
right in front of the whole class,
makes me feel
like I'm not wearing any clothes.

BOSTON

At least a few times a year,
Father takes the whole family
on his "Annual Tour of Boston."
He used to be a taxi driver,
so it's a pretty good tour.

We climb into the station wagon
and cruise along the curves of the Charles River
to get to the heart of downtown.
Father tailgates. Mother backseat drives.
My sister and I hunt for the letters of the alphabet.

Father steers past the Old North Church,
Bunker Hill Monument,
and the pier where the Boston Tea Party happened.
My sister and I thumb wrestle in the backseat.

He points out an apartment on Bowdoin Street
where John Kennedy used to live.
He shows us Longfellow's house,
and Paul Revere's,
but the house my sister and I want to see most
is the one Father lived in when he was a little boy,

an old brick building on Myrtle Street
with "28½" written in stained glass above the door.

We stop for lunch in Little Italy at The European,
where Father took Mother on their first date.
"If you eat your carrots," he tells us,
"you'll grow hair on your chest!"
We've heard him say this hundreds of times
but it still makes my sister and me giggle.

We take a ride on the swan boats,
then stroll through the Public Gardens.
Father holds Mother's hand.
My sister and I search for all the spots
we've read about so many times
in *Make Way for Ducklings*.

At least a few times a year,
Father takes the whole family
on his "Annual Tour of Boston,"
but today when he took us
and my sister wasn't there,
the backseat seemed huge
and I spent most of the time
just trying not to cry.

LIKE ALICE

Sister says
she feels like Alice
trapped in Wonderland,
forced to take potions
and pills.

DRINK ME
makes her
head shrink.
EAT ME
makes it grow.

She wishes
she could get small enough
to float right out through the keyhole
of that six-inch-thick iron door
on a sea of her own tears.

"Isn't that what Alice did
in that Disney movie?
Isn't it?" she demands. "Alice was the one
with the ruby slippers. Wasn't she?"
Sister stomps her foot,

then she clicks her heels together three times
and whirls and twirls
like she's caught in a cyclone
until she collapses onto her bed,
curling up into a tight fist.

She opens her mouth to scream,
but no sound comes out.
And when I sit
on the edge of her bed
and reach out to stroke her hair,

she doesn't even notice.

ONE BIT OF DIFFERENCE

When I used to wake up frightened
in the middle of the night,
Sister would come
and sit on the edge of my bed
until I fell back to sleep.

Now no one is there
in the middle of the night,
no one for me
and no one for her.

There's no one for her
night *or* day
and it doesn't matter how much
I want to help
because even when I sit
on the edge of her bed
she doesn't know I'm there.

Nothing I do or say makes
one
bit
of difference.

TIRED

I'm tired
of having a crazy sister.
I'm tired of being
the sister of a crazy person.

I'm tired of visiting her in the hospital,
and of all those zombies
wandering the corridors
mumbling gibberish.

I'm tired of this lump in my throat
and this ache in my chest
and these knots that gnaw
at my stomach.

I'm tired of having nobody to talk to.
I'm tired of walking to school alone
and of walking home from school
alone

and of crying
till my eyes look like

I've walked
into a door.

I'm tired of my parents fighting so loud
that the whole block trembles
and then
of the awful silence.

I'm tired of not knowing
when my sister will get well
or if she ever
will be well again.

I'm tired of not having fun,
and of not getting any of the attention,
and of things not being
like they used to be

and of things being like they are
and of Father never hugging me and
of Mother always wanting me to rub her back
and I'm tired of rubbing her back and

I'm tired of listening to her weep
through my bedroom wall at night
and to Father
snoring right through it.

I'm tired of trying to cheer her up
and of trying to convince her
that my sister doesn't really mean
all those nasty things she says.

I'm tired of not believing in God
or in miracles or in angels
or in fairies
or fairy godmothers.

I'm tired of being thirteen
and of not being twelve anymore
and of wanting to help my sister
and of not being able to help.

LAST NIGHT THEY FOUND
AUDREY BECKER'S MOTHER

Face down in the pond.
She'd been missing a week.
People said
she'd gone nuts.
Now she's dead.

There's this thought
I can't shake from my head.
No matter
how hard
I try.

There's this thought.

BICYCLE RIDE

I glide out
onto the fresh paved road
and pedal hard
until the wind
lifts my hair
off my shoulders
and a trap door
at the back of my skull
swings open,
letting the gloom
swirl out.

MY GUIDANCE COUNSELOR

On Monday
I told Mr. G
how depressed and lonely I was.
He told me
no one wants to make friends
with someone who looks miserable.

He said I ought to try
putting a smile on my face.
Even a pretend one
would do.
I thought this was idiotic,
but I was desperate.

All week long,
I forced a grin onto my lips.
It felt painted on,
tight, frozen.
I was sure everyone knew
it was an act,

but then
someone smiled back.
They hadn't noticed
my smile was a lie.
Somebody else
said hello.

I couldn't believe
how easily I'd fooled them
and even fooled myself,
because I found
that the more I smiled,
the more I really felt like smiling.

On Friday,
Sarah invited me
to her slumber party.
So I guess maybe Mr. G
isn't such an idiot
after all.

SLUMBER PARTY LEVITATION

When it's
my turn, I lie
down on the rug and the
girls kneel around me in a hushed
circle.

They slip
their forefingers
underneath me and then,
on a whispered count of three, they
lift up.

For those
few seconds that
I'm floating in the air,
I don't think about my sister
at all.

IN GYM CLASS

Ever since her mother died,
no one seems to know
what to say
to Audrey.

So they mostly
just act like she isn't there.
At least they've stopped calling her
Odd Audrey.

Today in gym class
I knew no one would choose her
to be their partner,
so I asked her if she'd be mine.

We'll never
talk about it,
but Audrey and I
have a lot in common.

OVER IT

Walking home from school with Sarah
to do our homework
together,
I see Molly and Kate up ahead

and for the first time since they dumped me,
I don't feel a thing.
I don't even wish
they'd get hit by a truck anymore.

WHY SISTER DOESN'T CROSS MY MIND ON THE WAY HOME FROM HORSENECK BEACH

I'm tucked
in the soft leather
of the backseat
between Sarah
and her big brother Sean.
Headlights slice
through the darkness
that surrounds us.
Sarah's asleep.
Sean's bare arm
rests against mine.
With his parents right there
in the front seat,
he inches his hand under my shirt
onto my stomach,
then waits,
to see if I'll push it away.
When I don't,
he begins
stroking my skin

very lightly
with long, warm fingers,
back and forth,
back and forth,
and his parents are right there
in the front seat.
I stare straight ahead
into the rearview mirror
at my own gleaming eyes
while he rubs my stomach
till I'm dizzy,
and he's slipping his hand
slowly up,
up
and up,
and now his wrist
grazes the bottom of my bra
and I can't breathe
when my hand brushes his thigh
and my fingertips are singed
and his parents are right there
in the front seat
and we pull up
in front of my house.

I DIDN'T NEED TO WORRY

This afternoon,
before Sarah came over
to spend the night
for the first time,
I started thinking about
her sleeping in my sister's bed.

I didn't want her to.
It just didn't feel
right, somehow.
I spent a long time
trying to figure out how to tell Sarah
without hurting her feelings.

Turns out I didn't need to worry.

A few minutes ago,
when it was time to go to bed
and I was just about to blurt it out,
Sarah turned pinker than my bedroom
and said she'd rather
sleep on the rug.

She said the idea
of sleeping in a crazy person's bed
kind of gave her the creeps.
I probably should have offered
to sleep in my sister's bed
and given *my* bed to Sarah.

But I didn't.

MRS. ZOLLI

My art teacher
changes my life
when she sees me admiring
her gleaming Nikon
with the fancy long lens
and asks:
"How'd you like to borrow it
for the weekend?"

KODAK MOMENT

Smile for the camera.
Say "cheese."
Try and look
like your old, sane self
for just one second.

Please.

IN THE DARKROOM

It's so
quiet and red,
deep red,
as I slip
the blank sheet
into the chemicals
and watch
your face
fade slowly up
out of redness,
smiling
a deep red
healthy
smile at me,
and I
smile back,
feeling like
a magician.

THE NEW BOY

Every day
he sits at a table
by himself
across the cafeteria
and watches me.

And every day
I eat lunch
with Sarah and the other girls,
pretending I don't notice him
while my heart does a fifty-yard dash.

Sarah says Betsy told her that Ava said
his name is Jim or John
or something like that.

Whoever he is,
I think I'm in love.

THE BEST MAY 2ND OF MY LIFE

I'm on my way in to the cafeteria
when Cathy Butler
shoves past
knocking all my books and folders
to the ground

I kneel down to gather them up
and he's suddenly beside me
the new boy
kneeling right there next to me
helping me pick up my things

he's smiling at me
saying hello
asking me my name
telling me his
asking if he can sit with me at lunch

I'm saying okay
and then we're together at a little table
and we're talking
and every single atom of me feels
so wide awake it almost hurts

and I'm thinking
he looks even better
close up like this
sitting right across from me
with our knees nearly touching

he's asking for my number
and I'm saying 555-6387
and I'm feeling all lit up
like a jar filled
with a thousand fireflies

I *am* in love with the new boy
in love with every
single
atom
of John

HE CALLS ME EVERY NIGHT

I don't
even know
what we talk about

I just listen
to the sound of his voice
and to his laugh

and to the sound
of him listening
to me

I bet *he* doesn't even know
what we talk about
either

but every night
when the telephone rings
a bell goes off inside me too

MAYBE I WON'T BE
NEEDING A DOG AFTER ALL

This morning
I showed my parents
the photographs I took with my teacher's camera.
They especially liked the ones of my sister.

Tonight
after dinner
they handed me a box
all wrapped up in silver paper with a big blue bow.

I opened it
and found a brand new
35-millimeter camera
with six rolls of film.

And it's
not
even
my birthday!

HER SELF-PORTRAIT

When I arrive,
Sister's sitting on the edge of her bed,
staring at the wall
with tears streaming down her cheeks.
But when I show her my new camera,
she brightens.
"And it's not even your birthday!" she says.
I grin and tell her,
"That's just what *I* said when I saw it."

"Can I hold it?" she asks,
and for a second I consider saying no,
flashing back to the Monopoly board
flying through the air,
but then I see the light in her eyes
and remember how excited
she always used to get about things.
I haven't seen that look in so long.

I place the camera in her hands
and then I show her the photos I took of her
with Mrs. Zolli's camera.
"They don't look a bit like me,"
she complains.

"Can I take a picture?
Is there any film in here?
Let me take one.
Come on. I'll show you how it's done."

I love seeing her like this.
"Go ahead," I say.
Her mirror's been covered
with a sheet for months,
but now with one swift tug she yanks it down.
She seems startled at first by what she sees.
Then she arranges her hair
neatly behind one ear.
She aims, moves the camera carefully
to just below her chin,
and shoots.

"That," she says smiling proudly,
with her eyes still fixed on her reflection,
"was a good one."
Then she turns and snaps one of me,
catching me off guard,
catching me so happy to have finally made
a difference.

AFTER SCHOOL

I'm walking home with John
to introduce him to my parents.
I've got to
or they won't let us
go to the movies together
this Saturday afternoon.

Half a block from my house,
we hear a man and a woman shouting.
John says, "Wow. Listen to those two go at it."
I think to myself:
I *have* been listening to them,
for months now.

I slow my pace,
but there's no way out.
Their voices grow louder
as we head up the front walk,
and now
John knows.

I have a key,
but I ring the bell
and the fighting stops abruptly.
When the door swings open
my father's standing there,
shoving his hair off his forehead.

He offers his hand, saying, "Hey, come on in."
I say, "John, Dad. Dad, John."
My father forces a smile and says,
"Cookie's mom really wants to meet you too.
But she's got a pretty bad headache right now.
Maybe she'll be down later on."

John smiles back, "I hope so."
And then,
right in front of my father,
he reaches over
and takes my hand
in his.

FIRST DATE

Our eyes
are glued to the
screen, but our thoughts are glued
to the spot where our elbows are
touching.

BECAUSE OF JOHN

I wasn't pretty
until John said I was.
He thinks I'm pretty
even when I've been crying.

I told him about my sister.
He didn't care.
I mean he was sorry she was sick
but he still likes me.

I wasn't pretty
until John said I was,
but now
I am.

AFTER THE DANCE

Walking home
together,
our fingers laced,
a thrilling silence
connects us.

When we turn
onto my block,
he draws me in
among the elms
on the McNamaras' lawn.

There
hidden from the prying light of the moon
he asks me
with his eyes,
and I'm just about to answer

when the headlights
on my parents' station wagon
blind us
and my mother calls out:
"Cookie? Is that you?"

SECRET RENDEZVOUS
AT THE FULL MOON CAFÉ

We planned it
so carefully.

Even synchronized
our watches.

Then

last night
at the stroke of midnight

he looked at the moon
through *his* bedroom window

and at the exact same moment

I looked at the moon
through *mine*.

AFTER THE PARTY
ON FRIDAY NIGHT

The whole walk home,
I'm wondering if he'll kiss me
and wondering what it will feel like
if he does.

Halfway there,
he slips his arm around my waist
and I slip mine
around his.

We move on
through the quiet streets,
hip pressed lightly to hip,
falling into a smooth rhythm.

As we near my house,
he leads me into a pool of dark
that lies just beyond
the glare of the streetlight

and suddenly presses
his lips onto mine,
melting us
together

till
he pulls back
and looks into my eyes
saying, "Maybe we shouldn't have done that."

Then
he grins
and kisses me
again.

WITH A CLICK

hiking
on a sunny Saturday
with my camera
and my boyfriend

we wander through Rock Meadow
the soft grass waving
bees humming in the wildflowers
click

he finds a heart-shaped stone
tucks it into my pocket
leans against a willow tree
watching me

there's something about
those eyes
those darkest lashes
click

that face
that hair
those warmest lips
click

my boyfriend
watching me
through the feathery leaves of the willow
click

looking at me in that way he does
with that smile in his eyes
that shine
that way that makes me love him

that look of his
of my boyfriend's
captured forever
with a *click*

PSYCH WARD RULE #37

When I show my sister
the photos of John,
she whistles.
She wants to know *all* about him.
So I tell her everything,
and for a few perfect minutes,
we forget where we are.

But then she starts scratching her head
so hard it hurts to watch, and blurts out,
"Hey, don't you want to hear
about Jake and me?"
"Who's Jake?" I ask.
"He just got here last week," she says.
"Best-looking lunatic I've ever seen."

She says she's got a big crush on Jake.
And Jake's got one back on her.
"But it doesn't do us any good,"
she sighs. "There's no p.c. allowed."
"What's p.c.?" I ask.
"Physical contact," she says.
"Psych Ward Rule #37."

"Don't feel so bad," I say.
"Mom and Dad won't let John and me
have any p.c. either."
We burst out laughing,
but on the inside
I'm wondering if my sister
will ever be able to have a boyfriend again.

E.R.

Sarah tells me her cousin Lisa
took something
that made her see
these little tiny bloody men
peeking out at her from the bushes,
and a gigantic praying mantis
chasing her down the street.

Lisa said it was like having
a really scary movie
playing right inside her head,
and that even when she closed her eyes
it wouldn't go away.
She ended up
in the emergency room.

I tell Sarah I wouldn't try that stuff
even if someone
paid me a million dollars.
I wouldn't want to do something
that might land me in a room
right down the hall
from my sister.

MEETING SISTER

My sister
wants to meet my boyfriend.
And she won't stop bugging me about it.
"What's the matter?"
she keeps asking.
"Are you ashamed of me?"

I finally make myself tell John.
I say I'll understand completely
if he doesn't want to.
I'm secretly hoping
he'll refuse.
But he doesn't.

We ride the subway
over to the hospital.
John jumps
when the heavy iron door of the ward locks
KACHUNGGGG
behind us,

but when he meets Sister,
he handles it pretty well,
even when she whacks herself hard
on the side of her head
and tells us she's trying to kill the fly
that's buzzing around in her brain.

Aside from this,
she manages to seem almost normal.
Charming, even.
She's working so hard
not to embarrass me.
I could kiss her.

On the way home
John says,
"I like her. I like your sister."
And I love him more
at this moment
than I've ever loved him before.

SISTER'S VOICES

The voices came whispering again
last night, while she was lying in her bed.
She thought she heard them say her name and then

their laughter rustled deep inside her head.
They didn't seem to know she was awake,
listening to every word they said.

She tried to block them out, but couldn't make
them go away. The voices asked her why
she'd lost her mind. Her hands began to shake.

She heard them mention shock treatments, and sigh
Their murmurs kept her up all night, and then
a silence fell when sunlight filled the sky . . .

Today the voices will be gone, but when
evening falls and she lies in her bed,
she'll hear them come whispering again.

SISTER SAYS IT'S NOT SO BAD

She says
it sort of feels like
someone's wrapping her up
in his long arms,
holding her tight,
calming her,
cooling her,
all through the night,
settling her,
soothing her,
keeping her safe,
like a second self,
like a faithful friend,

her jacket of white.

SHOCK

Will they
strap down her wrists
and ankles to the table?

Will they
shove something hard into her mouth
to keep her from biting her tongue?

Will they
turn up the dial with icy smiles
just like in the movies?

Will they
flip the switch,
slamming an arch into her back?

Will she
forget everything
for a while after this?

Will she
even forget
to be crazy?

AFTER SHOCK

Remember the time
we pulled over
by the side of the road
and Dad gave us lumps of sugar
to feed some horses?

Nope.

Remember the cartoon characters
on the wallpaper
in our bedroom
when we lived on Harvard Terrace?

Nope.

Remember that little dog
we used to give our Cheerios to?

Nope.

Remember me?

HAIR TODAY, THERE TOMORROW

Remember last spring
when Mom finally gave you
the short haircut you wanted
and tucked your freshly snipped ponytail
into that plastic bag?

We wondered why.

The next morning at breakfast
there it was: wrapped up into
a neat round bun on Mom's head,
hiding the spot
where her hair was thinning.

I knew what would happen
if I looked at you,
but I couldn't help it.
You made your eyes wide as two fried eggs,
and we burst into hysterics.

Remember?

GOING FOR THE GOLD

Remember when Mom
went through her "Gold Leaf Period"?
She had that stack
of thin booklets
filled with sheets of foil
made of real actual gold.

Remember how she went around
gluing it on to everything?

We had gold-leafed doorknobs,
gold-leafed Kleenex dispensers,
gold-leafed light switches,
and gold-leafed leaves on the plastic flowers
in our gold-leafed flower pots.

We even had a gold-leafed
toilet seat.
Remember?

We'd had that toilet seat
for a couple of months
when you and I noticed
that the gold leaf
was starting to wear off.

So we checked each other's bottoms
to see if they were glittering
and had a fit of gold-leafed giggles.

You remember that.

You do!

FINALLY

I fly home
from the hospital
to share the news
with my parents:

"She *knew* me today.
She knew who I was
and I knew her, too.
She was there. *Really* there.
We talked about dreams.
She braided my hair.
We sat side by side
and played 'Heart and Soul.'

Today, I hated to leave."

I hug my parents
and they hug me back,
holding tight
like feathers to the wing of a bird.

GIRLS' NIGHT IN

Mother's friends
are over tonight
and I'm sitting
at the top of the stairs
listening
to the tinkling
of their voices,
the gentle *flup*
of the cards being shuffled,
the muffled jingling
of coins tossed onto the silk tablecloth,
and the best sound of all:
my mother's long lost laugh.

MEMORIAL DAY

No school today.
Mother's gone to shop the sales.
Father's stationed in front of the TV,
cheering for the Red Sox.
I plop down next to him on the couch.
He looks over at me and says,
"I thought you hated baseball."
"You're right," I say. "I think watching baseball
is about as interesting as watching a faucet drip."
He laughs, long and deep,
and then, he switches off the TV.

Just like that.

"Come on," he says.
"Let's you and me
go get some fish and chips over at Kelly's."

It's lucky he's holding my hand
on the way to the car
or I'd probably just float up
into the sky
like a balloon.

TONIGHT

I'm tucked
between my mother and father,
snuggling on the couch
under the quilt that Grandma Ruthie made,
watching an old movie on television,
eating popcorn.

And tonight,
for once,
it feels okay
to just be

three.

DR. MILTON SILVER

Somehow
Sister and I
start talking about our dentist
and she confesses
that whenever she's alone with him
in his office
he tells her
she's the prettiest
of the two sisters.

I gasp when I hear this
and confess
that whenever *I'm* alone with him
in his office
he tells me
I'm the prettiest
of the two sisters.

And then we start laughing
and we can't stop
and we clutch each other
and laugh and laugh
until visiting hour's over

and I think to myself
that this moment
was definitely
worth
all the drilling.

IN THE VISITING ROOM

The four of us sit down
to play Scrabble.
Father puts down HOTEL.
Mother puts down TIRED.
I put down WHEN.

It's my sister's turn.
She fiddles
with her letters
on the little wooden rack
trying them first one way

then another
for what seems like a long time.
Finally,
she smiles slyly
and puts down SPIDOSAL.

"Spidosal?" Father says.
"Spidosal . . ." Mother says.
"What's that mean?" I say.
"Fifty extra points, that's what!"
Sister says.

Father raises an eyebrow.
Then he winks at my sister
and puts down HOOKIBOP.
"Not bad," she says.
"Not bad at all."

Mother peers at her
over the top of her reading glasses,
then she grins and puts down QUEEB.
"That's not a word!" Sister says.
"It is now," Mother says.

My sister gives her a high five.
It's my turn.
I look around the table
at my whole family
and put down BETTER.

AUTHOR'S NOTE

The poems you have just read were inspired by the events that took place when the older of my two sisters had a nervous breakdown. I was going on thirteen at the time, and I looked up to and admired my sister, who was nineteen. Until then she'd never exhibited any disturbing behavior.

When she broke down on that Christmas Eve, she had to be placed in a psychiatric ward and was diagnosed as manic-depressive. I was terrified by this illness that had suddenly transformed my sister into a stranger. But I hid this fear from everyone, only letting down my guard in the pages of my journal. Being able to pour out all my feelings onto those clean white pages every night helped me to survive.

My sister was released from the hospital after a few months. Although she has had to be hospitalized several times since then, she has been able to lead a productive and satisfying life. She married, earned a master's degree in library science, and worked as a public librarian for over twenty years. Now she spends her time doing volunteer work and taking classes in writing, drawing, and African literature. She still sees a psychiatrist and takes medication to keep her illness under control.

As for myself, I still look up to and admire my big sister. And ever since that difficult time when she first got sick, I've continued to write in journals. I have hundreds of them, stored away in a closet. A few years ago my interest in writing led me to enroll in a poetry class at UCLA, taught by Myra Cohn Livingston. One day Myra asked us to write a poem using falling rhythms, which lend themselves to serious themes. When I placed my pen to the blank page, out came "Hospitalized," an intense poem about having to visit my sister in the psychiatric ward.

I felt insecure about sharing these private feelings with the outside world for the first time. But Myra took me aside after class and encouraged me to write more poems about my sister's illness. "Poems like this," she said, "would be helpful to anyone who has a family member with a problem that's throwing the rest of the family off-kilter."

I was scared to begin delving into my disturbing memories, but gradually I began to write more and more poems about my sister. This was the beginning of *Stop Pretending*.

Naturally, I was concerned about how my sister would feel about my writing this book. But when I told her about it, she was extremely supportive of my efforts. She says she hopes the book will be used to open up discussions about mental illness. She wishes people had a better understanding of this disease, so they would treat its victims with more compassion.

Mental illness affects millions of families, and it can be very scary and confusing. If you are worried about your own mental health or the health of a family member or friend, here are some numbers you can call to get help:

MIND
15–19 Broadway
London
EI5 4BQ
(020) 8519 2122
contact@mind.org.uk

SANE
City Side House
40 Alder Street
London
EI IEE
(020) 7375 1002
sane@saneline.org

The Samaritans
10 The Grove
Slough
Berkshire
SLI IQP
(0175) 3216 500
admin@samaritans.org.uk

ALSO BY SONYA SONES

What my mother doesn't know:
A story of love and confusion

My name is Sophie.
This book is about me.
It tells
the heart-stoppingly riveting story
of my first love.
And also of my second.
And, okay, my third love, too.

It's not that I'm boy crazy.
It's just that even though
I'm almost fifteen
I've been having sort of a hard time
trying to figure out the difference
between love and lust.

It's like
my mind
and my body
and my heart
just don't seem to be able to agree
on anything.

Truthful, touching, funny and sad, this is Sonya Sones's
second novel in verse, following *Stop Pretending: what
happened when my big sister went crazy.*

About the author

As a teenager Sonya Sones spent hours pouring her private thoughts and feelings into journals. Her passion for writing, drawing and photography led her to begin making animated films when she was seventeen. She studied filmmaking in college, and went on to teach animation, make films for public television, and edit movies in Hollywood. She lives with her husband and two children in California.

Sonya Sones can be reached at SonyaSones@aol.com